With every
good wish
from

Joanna Bogle
St George's
March 2012

BLESSED JOHN PAUL THE GREAT

JOANNA BOGLE

Blessed John Paul the Great

Illustrations by
Kati Teague

ST PAULS

Other titles in this series:

St Paul – Friend of Jesus
St John Vianney – The Curé of Ars
St Thérèse of Lisieux – The Little Flower
Blessed John Henry Newman – Heart Speaks to Heart

ST PAULS Publishing
187 Battersea Bridge Road, London SW11 3AS, UK
www.stpaulspublishing.com

Copyright © ST PAULS 2011
ISBN 978-0-85439-819-5

A catalogue record is available for this book from
the British Library.

Set by TuKan DTP, Stubbington, Fareham, UK
Printed by Bishops Printers, Portsmouth

ST PAULS is an activity of the priests and brothers
of the Society of St Paul who proclaim the Gospel
through the media of social communication.

Introduction

Many people have heard about the great John Paul. He was the Pope who came from Poland, and he changed the course of history.

He had a special love of Our Lady and taught people all around the world to love her too.

John Paul was very brave; someone in St Peter's Square tried to kill him by shooting him and he almost died. But he forgave his attacker and went on travelling and teaching people about Christ.

He brought young people together in great crowds and spoke to them in a new and fresh way, helping everyone to understand that we can do nothing without God.

This is the story of his life.

The Wojtila family lived in Poland, in a town called Wadowice. They were thrilled when a new baby was born on 18th May 1920. They named him Karol after his father. (Karol is the Polish way of saying "Charles".)

Karol had an older brother, Edmund. They had nicknames for each other – Edmund was "Mundek" and Karol was "Lolek". There had been a sister too, but she died before Karol was born.

Karol's parents taught him about Poland, about the country's long history, its saints, kings and heroes. Most of all, they told him about the fact that Polish people were always loyal Catholics, always close to Jesus Christ and to the Church.

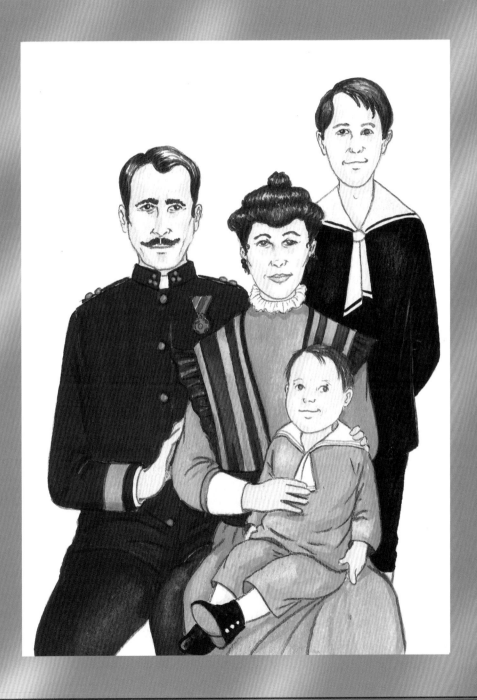

When Karol was still a young boy, there came great sadness. His mother, who had never been very well, died. His older brother Mundek, who had become a doctor and gone to work in a hospital, also became ill and died.

Karol and his father were left all alone. They prayed together every day before a big crucifix and his father explained to him that Jesus knew all about sadness and suffering. They loved each other and cared for each other.

All his life, Karol would remember how sometimes he would wake in the night and see his father quietly praying.

Karol worked hard at school, and also enjoyed sports, especially football.

He had lots of friends, some were Catholics and some were Jewish. He often played in the Jewish football team.

Karol loved to serve at Mass, and often stopped off at the church on his way to school. He had a special devotion to Mary, and prayed to her every day.

Karol and his father moved to the city of Krakow so that Karol could go to University. He loved books and poetry, acting and the theatre. He also loved Polish history, Polish songs and music.

While he was still a student, the Second World War started and Poland was invaded by Nazi Germany. All Poland's universities were closed. Polish people could no longer study, nor go to theatres or hear Polish poetry. The Nazis rounded up Jewish people and took them away to be killed. These were terrible days.

During the war, Karol worked in a stone quarry and at a chemical factory. It was hard work and there was not much food to eat. At this time Karol's father, who by now was old, died.

Karol and his friends wanted to keep Polish poetry and plays and music alive. They worked together to put on plays in people's homes and held secret gatherings to read aloud Polish poems.

One night, whilst travelling home, Karol was badly hurt in a road accident.

Every day when he prayed, Karol asked Mary to help him make the big decisions in his life. He wanted to do whatever God asked of him. Slowly, he knew what it was that he should do. He would become a priest, and serve God in that way for the rest of his life.

The Nazis had forbidden the Church in Poland to ordain any more priests. But the Bishop gathered the young men together secretly, and they went to his house to pray and study. If they had been discovered, they might have been shot.

The war ended, but, for Poland, it was not a happy time. Instead of the Germans, Poland was now run by the Communist Russians. They put in a government of their own choosing.

It seemed as though Poland would never be a free country. The Communists did not think that people should believe in God. They did not want the Church to flourish. They started to make all sorts of restrictions.

The Polish people had been brave during the war. Now they had to be brave again in this new situation. In 1946, Karol was ordained a priest. He was glad to serve God in Poland, at a time when people most needed priests.

Father Karol was a good priest. The young people loved him. He went hiking and canoeing with them.

The Communists did not want priests to teach young people about God.

So, on their hiking trips, the young people did not let anyone know they had a priest with them. They just called Father Karol "Uncle". They loved to hear him talk about Christ, and about how to live the Christian way, and how to pray. He celebrated Mass for them out in the open air. They would remember these happy times all their lives.

Father Karol soon realised that God had other and bigger plans for him. The Pope appointed him to be Archbishop of Krakow. He was still quite young, but Poland needed energetic Bishops to help people to be good Catholics. These were very difficult days under Communism.

The Government would not allow a church to be built in the big new town of Nowa Huta. When the people gathered for Mass, the police came and sent them away. Archbishop Karol stood firm. He insisted that the people had a right to have a church.

Finally, after years of campaigning, they were able to build one. Everyone helped. Archbishop Karol and all the people were so happy when they finally had a great new church, which he blessed with hundreds of people gathered joyfully together.

Archbishop Karol had many duties. He helped poor people. He preached and taught. He went to Rome to take part in the big Vatican Council, which had been called by Pope John XXIII, and was continued by the next Pope, Paul VI. When he came home, he taught the people of Krakow about the ideas and plans of the Council.

The Communist government was worried about him because he helped so many people to know about God. They had spies watching him. They listened to his sermons and made reports on everything he did. They tried to make trouble for him.

It was not an easy time to be a Bishop, but Archbishop Karol was busy and cheerful. He knew that God and Our Lady would take care of things, and he prayed and worked hard and urged everyone to be brave and to be united in the Church.

In 1967, Archbishop Karol was made a Cardinal, which meant that he had even more duties and responsibilities.

In 1978, Pope Paul VI died, and all the Cardinals went to Rome to elect a new Pope. They chose a good man, who took the name John Paul. Sadly, he was not very well, and died after 33 days as Pope.

So, all the Cardinals had to meet in Rome again. This time they chose Archbishop Karol Wojtila. He was elected Pope! It was the first time there had ever been a Polish Pope.

He took the name John Paul II, and for his motto, "*Totus Tuus*", dedicating his work as Pope to Our Lady, saying, "I am all yours".

The Communist government back in Poland was very, very worried, but all the Catholic Polish people were very, very happy.

Right from the start, John Paul II was a special and exciting Pope.

At his first big Mass as Pope he told everyone, "Do not be afraid!" "Open wide the doors to Christ!"

All the world knew that it was difficult to be a Catholic in Poland. When this Polish Pope spoke so clearly and bravely, they listened. He reminded people that Jesus Christ should be at the centre of their lives. He was strong and cheerful, and he went into the streets of Rome and talked to people.

All his life, Pope John Paul II had lived simply. He never bothered about smart clothes. When he was given new shoes or good clothes, he often gave them away to the poor.

As Pope, he lived simply too. In his room, he had small, old pictures of his parents and his brother Mundek. He still used an old prayer book that his father had given him. He did not want to be grand or important, he was warm and friendly with everyone.

People from all over the world wrote to him asking him to pray about their worries: people who were ill, a family who longed to have a baby, children who were victims of war. The letters were put in his chapel and he prayed for all these people.

He had always loved the Rosary, and, as Pope he still said the Rosary every day, just as he had done all his life.

John Paul badly wanted to make a visit to Poland. The Communist government did not want that at all, but, in the end, they had to agree to it. So John Paul, the Polish Pope, went to Poland.

All the people came out on to the streets to greet him and cheer him – they decorated their homes with flags and banners, they sang and shouted for joy. The whole country rejoiced!

Pope John Paul celebrated Mass in the open air, right in the middle of Warsaw, the capital city. He prayed, "May the Holy Spirit descend upon this land, and renew it!" The Communists knew – everyone knew – that, from now on, things in Poland would be different.

There were dangers for the Pope. One morning in St Peter's Square, on the Feast of Our Lady of Fatima, while he was with the crowds of people, a shot rang out. The Pope slumped back, shot in the stomach. Blood poured out – the Pope was almost dead. They rushed him to hospital. Everyone prayed.

Many years before, at Fatima in Portugal, Our Lady had appeared to three children. She had shown them a vision of a Pope, dressed in white, who was attacked and slumped down in St Peter's Square.

By a miracle, the Pope recovered. He had dedicated his life to Our Lady, and now she had saved him. The bullet should have killed him.

When he was fully well, Pope John Paul went to Fatima. Thousands of people gathered to pray with him. He placed the bullet that had nearly killed him, into the crown on her statue.

Pope John Paul travelled all over the world to teach people about Jesus Christ, to encourage them to be good Christians. Everywhere, huge crowds gathered, and there was joy and singing. Whenever he arrived in a country, the first thing he did was to kneel down and kiss the ground.

He spoke against war, and he urged people to be kind and generous to one another. He taught about the importance of families, and teaching children the Christian faith. He taught especially about God's forgiveness – the Divine Mercy. He had learned about this from a Polish nun, Sister Faustina.

He went to a synagogue, and showed that Jews and Christians should be friends together always.

In Rome, he chose Cardinal Joseph Ratzinger
to be one of his special helpers.
He asked Cardinal Ratzinger to help prepare
a new Catechism, so that people everywhere
would know what the Church taught.

John Paul taught people
about the importance
of the Rosary, and
he added five new
Mysteries to it. There
had traditionally been
the Joyful, Sorrowful,
and Glorious Mysteries,
and now he added the
Luminous Mysteries – the
Mysteries of Light.

Meanwhile, back in Poland, the people knew that they were no longer afraid. They formed a new group called SOLIDARITY. Finally, the Communists could not hold on to power any more. Freedom had come to Poland!

Other countries where the Communists had ruled were changing, too. The people gathered in big crowds and called for freedom.

The Polish Pope, dedicated to Our Lady, had changed the course of history.

Pope John Paul went back to Poland several times. The Polish people loved him: he was their hero!

Young people loved Pope John Paul. He spoke to them about Jesus Christ and showed them that being a Christian is a great and beautiful adventure. He taught that what matters is not money, or doing whatever we want. What matters is God – we will be truly happy when we follow His will. We can discover this by praying, and staying close to the Church.

Young people from all over the world came to hear John Paul in Rome. One day he said to them, "Let's do this again and again, in different parts of the world! We'll call it *World Youth Day!*"

Ever since then, there have been World Youth Days in different countries: in France, Spain, America, the Philippines, Germany and Australia among other places. Young people come together joyfully to pray, to make friends, to learn about Jesus Christ, and to build up peace in the world.

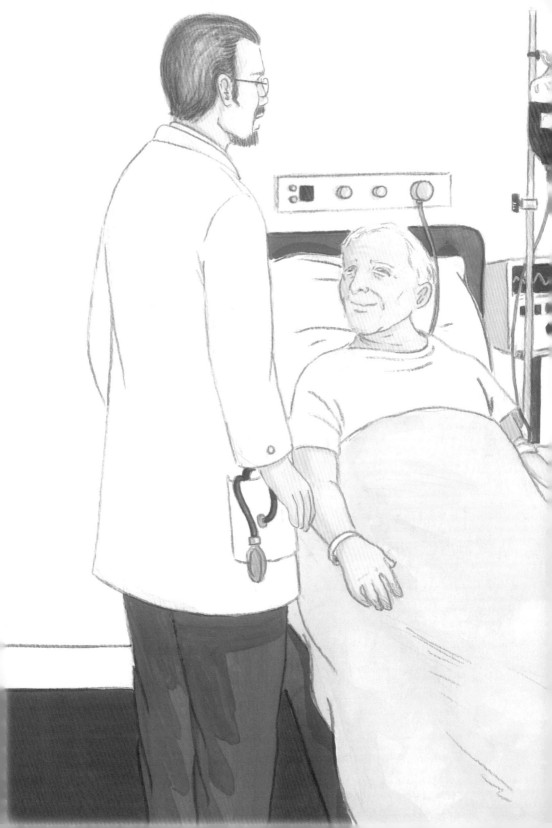

John Paul had always been fit and healthy and loved the outdoors. When he was younger he played football, but he also loved to ski and swim.

One day he became ill. He fell and broke his hip and the doctors then discovered that he had a tumour in his stomach.

After this he had an illness which would not go away. At first, it just made his hands shake and slowed down his movements. Little by little it made it impossible for him to move or speak easily. The illness is called Parkinson's Disease.

John Paul did not stop working. Even when he was ill and in pain, he went on teaching, and meeting people, and dealing with all his letters and other duties. He could not walk now. He had to be wheeled in a chair.

Every year, he had given people a special message and blessing at Easter, known as *Urbi et Orbi*, to the City and the World. Now he was very old and very ill, when he came to the window to greet everyone, his voice had gone. He could not speak. He tried, but it was no use.

He eventually stretched out his hand, and, very slowly, blessed everyone. The people applauded and called out greetings to let him know that they understood, and that they loved him.

Not long afterwards, the world was told that John Paul was dying. Among the great crowds who gathered in the Square outside St Peter's were huge numbers of young people, who all came to pray the Rosary. They wanted to be with John Paul in his final moments.

In his room within the Vatican, John Paul was calm and brave. Even though he was suffering and in pain, he was peaceful. He could hear all the people praying outside. Mass was celebrated by his bedside and he was given Holy Communion. He knew he was dying and said goodbye to all his closest friends.

"Let me go to my Father's house", he whispered, and gently, he slipped away to Heaven. It was the eve of Divine Mercy Sunday 2005.

People from all over the world came to John Paul's funeral. Cardinal Ratzinger celebrated the Mass in St Peter's Square. He showed people the window from where John Paul had given his last blessing. "Now he is standing at the window of our Father's house, and from there he sees us and blesses us", he said.

Young people in the square held banners saying "Thank you" to John Paul, and some saying "*Santo subito*", which means "Make him a saint soon!"

The Cardinals now had to elect a new Pope and they chose Cardinal Ratzinger, who took the name Benedict XVI. He became a wonderful Pope, and people loved him.

Six years after the great John Paul died, Pope Benedict declared him Blessed, the first step in making him a saint. His feast day is October 22nd, the day he took office as Pope.

Now that John Paul is in Heaven, we can ask him to pray for us.

John Paul was one of the greatest Popes in all the long history of the Catholic Church. He preached to millions and millions of people, and he changed the lives of many.

Today, and for years to come, his teachings will be studied. Already there are churches and schools and colleges named after him, and statues of him all around the world.

For young people, in particular, he is a special patron.

We will always remember that he taught everyone, "Do not be afraid!"

If we love God, and try to do his will, we need not be frightened of anything.

John Paul the Great, pray for us!

What were the nicknames Karol and his brother Edmund had for each other?

_____

_____

During the war Karol worked in a stone quarry. What did he and his friends do in their spare time?

_____

_____

In which year was he elected Pope and what is the meaning of his motto *"Totus Tuus"*?

_____

_____

What is the name of the new Mysteries Pope John Paul added to the rosary?

_____

_____

What is the name of the gathering of young people that first happened in Rome?

_____

_____

What were the last words Pope John Paul spoke before he died?

_____

_____

What is the name of the present Pope?

_____